STEP INTO THE CIRCLE

STEP INTO THE CIRCLE

EDITED BY TRENT THOMSON & AMY GREENE

BLAIR

Printed in the United States of America
Cover design by Laura Williams
Interior design by April Leidig

Blair is an imprint of Carolina Wren Press.

The mission of Blair/Carolina Wren Press is to seek out, nurture,
and promote literary work by new and underrepresented writers.

We gratefully acknowledge the ongoing support of general operations
by the Durham Arts Council's Annual Arts Fund and the N.C. Arts Council,
a division of the Department of Natural & Cultural Resources.

Library of Congress Control Number: 2019949131

Photos on page i and facing by Mallory Cash
Photo on page iii by Shawn Poynter

A VISION

If we will have the wisdom to survive,
to stand like slow-growing trees
on a ruined place, renewing, enriching it . . .
The abundance of this place,
the songs of its people and its birds,
will be health and wisdom and indwelling
light. This is no paradisal dream.
Its hardship is its possibility.

—Wendell Berry

CONTENTS

1   Introduction
AMY GREENE | PHOTOGRAPHS BY SHAWN POYNTER

9   Wendell Berry
SILAS HOUSE | PHOTOGRAPHS BY GUY MENDES & TANYA AMYX BERRY

21   Crystal Wilkinson
KAREN MCELMURRAY | PHOTOGRAPHS BY SAM STAPLETON

33   Ron Rash
WILEY CASH | PHOTOGRAPHS BY MALLORY CASH

41   Adriana Trigiani
AMY D. CLARK | PHOTOGRAPHS BY TIM C. COX & SHAWN POYNTER

51   Silas House
AMY GREENE | PHOTOGRAPHS BY C. WILLIAMS & TASHA THOMAS

59   George Ella Lyon
PATRICIA HUDSON | PHOTOGRAPHS BY SAM STAPLETON

69   Frank X Walker
DENTON LOVING | PHOTOGRAPHS BY ROBERT MORTON

79   Marie Junaluska
ANNETTE SAUNOOKE CLAPSADDLE | PHOTOGRAPHS BY WILL WARASILA

91   Lee Smith
JASON KYLE HOWARD | PHOTOGRAPHS BY MALLORY CASH

107   Contributors

INTRODUCTION

AMY GREENE

When Trent and I came to the place we would name Bloodroot Mountain, twenty-one forested acres with a timber-frame barn, it had gone for years uninhabited. In the woods where we climbed up through the trees, sun reached the ground in nickels and dimes. The shagbark trunks were twisted in vines. There were no voices. There were only wet weather streams over rocks. There were only leaves turned over and over, sifted and sorted by the hands of the wind.

It was a place we had been before and never before. We have always known the landscape of East Tennessee, narrow valleys made of ridges and creeks, ringed in mountains formed five hundred million years ago, once flooded by an ancient sea, the shellfish that swam those waters now fossilized in a layer of limestone sediment. We wondered as we walked the property about ancestral memory, if a person's connection to home might be inborn.

When we moved into the barn that became our studio, I sat writing with the door open, watching doves peck in the grass growing between the paving stones and among the locust saplings that had invaded the garden. They would come to the threshold and peer inside, molting feathers. For so long, it had been their domain.

Wild things had made their nests in the woodstove. Hickory nuts stored over field mouse winters rolled out from under the pie safe into dark

corners. Shed snake skins wrapped the iron bed legs. Up in the loft the floorboards were splattered white with the droppings of nesting swallows.

I suppose not many would have looked at Bloodroot Mountain and envisioned a place to live and work, maybe because it's harder somehow to see the beauty of the landscapes we know as we do ourselves, the geographies

that have toughened our feet. Home is sometimes too familiar. It's like when you hold your hand so close to your face that it blurs out of focus. The first time we encountered our land, Trent and I sensed more than saw what was possible. We glimpsed light in the depths of the pond's murk. We heard the lullaby creak of the barn boards. We considered that ginseng might grow on the steep, north-facing slopes. We began to dream that art could be formed out of the green silence.

We asked ourselves, what can be done here? Could this be a school of thought, an incubator for ideas? Could it be a beacon for progress in the wilderness? Could it be a quiet haven where artists find loud voices? The answer is always yes, if we make it so.

Yes, Bloodroot Mountain can be such a place. Yes, Appalachia can be such a place. It takes only seeing what's before us. It was the writer Lee Smith who first showed me. In my early twenties, I read her novel *Oral History* and thought, *I can write about my people and my place.* We and these mountains are worth something. It has largely been writers like Smith who have told the rest of the nation, *There's something going on here that counts.* They have said, *Look at our natural resources. Let's protect them. Look at our young. Let's lift them on our shoulders.* The ten writers featured here, by their words and deeds, have built a foundation not only for other writers, but for a whole culture to rise up on.

I think of all writers as seers, but perhaps Appalachian writers in particular, growing up in the hollows and coves, observers of the pasture hills and valleys, of our families across the supper table and our neighbors on their way to work.

It may be harder to see what's most familiar to us, but maybe the opposite is also true. You see more when you're invisible, when you've been overlooked. Maybe it's easier to dream up visions from the margins.

Trent and I had a vision for a place, which led to a book. It often happens that way.

WENDELL BERRY

SILAS HOUSE

Wendell Berry is driving us with the windows down, and the August wind is rushing into the cab of his truck. A working man's truck, complete with a metal toolbox and a coil of chain under my feet, two tobacco sticks on his dusty dashboard, and—best of all—his beloved border collie, Liz, in the back, her large brown eyes touching mine every time I look toward her. When I was first introduced to her, Wendell said, "This is Liz. I don't like to be without her or my pocketknife." Then Liz jumped into the pickup without having to be told and we took off.

Wendell is showing me the land he loves on the day before his eighty-fourth birthday. Most people might imagine rolling pastures with neat swirls of hay and shining thoroughbreds. But this is the man who wrote the masterpiece "The Peace of Wild Things" and he has seen to it that his land offers concord to the untamed. We are on a gravel road where the air grows green with leaf-light. On my side of the truck there is a steep bank rising skyward. On Wendell's side the land drops down toward the meandering stream called Cane Run, whose waters flow calmly against sandy banks but possess a music when they swirl about in the exposed roots of beech trees or stumble over small congregations of rocks. Most of the trees are thin, and when I notice this Wendell tells me that all of this land was once cleared to make way for tobacco fields in which he worked as a young man, just as I did as a child. "It's a gone way of life," he says as we remember the

beauty and misery of setting the plants, staking them, hanging the tobacco in the stifling, fragrant heat of the barns. We both recall the cold depths of a swimming hole after working in the fields all day. The camaraderie. The aunts on the setters, chattering over the groan of the tractor. I was once a twelve-year-old boy, beaming with pride as I drove the truck across the fields. Wendell was once a man in his early thirties, fists on his hips as he looked out at the tobacco planted across the bottomlands.

Despite being cleared as recently as fifty years ago, there are occasional elderly trees, too. I spy a sycamore that must be two or three hundred years old, and Wendell stops in the road so we can spend a moment with it. I am reminded of one of my favorite poems by him, "The Sycamore," and its lines: "In the place that is my own place, whose earth / I am shaped in and must bear, there is an old tree growing." The really interesting phrase to me there is "whose earth / I . . . must bear," and I think it reveals a lot about the man as well as the poet.

I sneak a glance at his clear blue eyes as they climb the branches of the sycamore, and there it is: grief. Wendell is a jovial man. He laughs heartily, tells bawdy tales and dirty jokes, and speaks often of love and contentment. He possesses much joy, but that somehow makes his constant grief even more noticeable. The sadness is not only in his eyes, but also on the backs of his hands. It rests across his shoulders. He is one of those people whose constant attention to joy reminds him, all the time, that there is much suffering in the world. And he is incredibly conscious of that pain, whether it is happening to farmers who have been systematically knocked out of work by big industry and the government, or mountainsides that are being obliterated, or the fact that a whole lot of people just don't pay any attention to the natural world at all.

Perhaps this is what we love most about him, our Wendell. It's what I love most, at least.

I also love that he has let these many acres grow wild. He points out a few experiments. There is a trinity of box elders, their leafy branches praising in the slight breeze. "I cut back some of the trees to give them light, and they've done very well," he says. He tells me stories of the land and its people—inseparable. All in all he and his wife, Tanya, now have 117 acres here. His people have known this land since his mother's great-great-grandfather and his father's great-grandfather. He and Tanya have already made arrangements for this land to become a natural conservancy as an agricultural conservation easement through the PACE (purchase of agricultural conservation easement) program, he tells me. "Eventually it'll be an old-growth forest," he says. This will take two hundred years, and although Berry knows he won't ever see it, he is pleased to know that someday it will exist, right here.

Back out of the holler, the tires of his truck hum on the pavement. The river flashes by through the thick trees on my right—sluggish and dark green in summertime. Then we are climbing a mountain even though we are at the edge of the bluegrass region. I'm surprised by how Appalachian it feels here since we are many miles west of the mountain range. "The difference is that in eastern Kentucky, you go up the mountain and then you go down it," Wendell explains. "But here you go up to the next ridge." At the top of the ridge is the little town of Port Royal, which possesses a couple of churches, a bank, and a restaurant where the parking lot is crowded with vehicles since it is noon. There is also the post office, which Wendell frequents quite often. Today he is mailing off eight letters. He tells me to wait in the truck, and he hops out like a teenager and bounds inside.

I am thinking how surreal it is to be going to the post office with one of my heroes. With one of the people who shaped me not only as a writer, but also as a person.

Wendell has allowed me much joy, but he's also filled me with grief. Both of those are good things, as it is wrong to go through the world blindly, to not take note of the destruction, of the suffering of others. We cannot be full people if we live blissfully ignorant. For many years now Wendell has been one of the people who has taken hold of our chins and turned them toward the beauty and the horror. They exist side by side in almost all of his work, and he has spent his career making us aware. There's a very good reason a recent documentary about him (in which he refused to appear on-screen) is called *Look and See*—this is how he has lived his life, and this is what he has taught so many of us. Bearing witness, however, brings along the sad knowledge that there are so many battles to fight and that we can never do enough. But Wendell has always tried his best to do his most, and he's asked the same of us.

Wendell has been one of the people who has taken hold of our chins and turned them toward the beauty and the horror.

About four years after my first novel was published, I received a letter from Wendell inviting me on a fact-finding mission. I was amazed that he knew who I was. In the letter he said that the form of coal mining known as mountaintop removal (MTR) was ravaging Eastern Kentuckians, and since our legislators were rubber-stamping the devastation, it was up to the state's artists to do something about it. He had planned two days of information gathering. Artists who attended would participate in small-plane flyovers so they could see the full breadth of the mining. They'd walk a healthy mountain with a local man who would show them its medicinal and food values. Finally, they would listen in to an open community meeting where people in the area would be invited to come tell their stories of living near MTR operations. Would I come along with them?

I had always identified myself as an environmentalist. I had grown up near a large strip mine that forever changed our community. For years I

lived in the noise and dust of the local mine. I saw the beloved ridge across from my childhood home reduced to rubble. I watched as our narrow road became domineered by overloaded coal trucks and stamped with the tracks of dozers. I knew what mining could do to a piece of land. But I was also raised in a family who had risen up out of poverty in large part due to coal. I knew the issue was complicated, but speaking out against coal was not: where I'm from one simply didn't do it, although this hadn't always been the case. During the bloody coal wars of the 1920s, Appalachians had gone to war with the coal companies for safer working conditions and better pay. Even when I was a child in the 1970s and 1980s, I was aware of the increasingly violent strikes that were happening. When I was in high school, more than two hundred people were arrested for civil disobedience while protesting for safer mines just over the West Virginia border, less than two hours from where I lived. But by the 2000s, the coal industry had largely accomplished its goal of ridding Appalachia of the unions and indoctrinating people with the belief that without coal, we had absolutely nothing else. They spent millions on campaigns to convince people that "Coal Keeps the Lights On" and that to even think of any other kind of economy was foolish. They flooded small-town festivals with free t-shirts and handed out coloring books at our local schools. The propaganda was constant and very smart in that it aligned coal with our identity—the most important thing to Appalachian people. To some degree I had become as brainwashed as everyone else around me, although I was disgusted daily by the environmental devastation I was seeing. I had woven environmental issues into my first three novels, especially my third one, in which three women lie down in front of bulldozers to protect their family land from strip miners. But as soon as I read Wendell's letter, I knew that I could no longer quietly think and write about the issue. I had to act.

Once I did the flyover, walked the mountain, and participated in the community meeting, I was fired up. For the next few years the issue of mountaintop removal would become my main concern after my family and my writing—and even took over the writing for a while. Wendell mobilized many artists in Kentucky to join forces, to witness what was happening and then report on it. He was at the forefront of bringing together writers, photographers, musicians, and other artists to make the issue more widely known. Our main goal was to let people know mountaintop removal was happening and then hope that they would join us in protesting. They did.

It would have been easier for all of us to turn a blind eye to what was happening. That is how we survive so much.

One time I went along with Wendell and several others, prepared to be arrested if our demand to meet with the governor of Kentucky went unheard. I watched as a lawyer's phone number was written in ink on Wendell's forearm. The governor talked to us briefly in the hallway but would not offer a sit-down meeting, and we refused to leave. The governor was too smart to have us arrested—he likely imagined the public outcry if Wendell Berry was led out of the state capitol in handcuffs—so he invited us to stay in his office. And so for three days Wendell and thirteen others stayed there.

That first night I have an image of him I will never forget: a jacket rolled up under his head as he lay on the marble floor of the governor's office, reading a ragged copy of a Shakespeare play. He was seventy-seven years old then. During that time I had known him about seven years but still could only bring myself to call him "Mr. Berry." I addressed him as such as he lay there and his eyes met mine. "Don't you think it's about time you called me Wendell?" he asked. Ever since, I have.

After three days of occupying the governor's mansion and becoming international news, we went out to greet the thousands of people who had congregated on the front steps of the capitol. When Wendell appeared at the podium, a roar rose from the crowd that caused goose bumps to run up and down the backs of my arms and tears to spring to my eyes.

The practice of mountaintop removal continues, but many more people know about it and oppose it because of the leadership of Wendell and those he called into action. It would have been easier for all of us to turn a blind eye to what was happening. That is how we survive so much. How, after all, could we get through the day if we thought of all the atrocities happening in the world at this moment? But Wendell held our feet to the fire and asked us to join him. We couldn't refuse him because we knew he was right. I'm grateful for the grief he gave to me. I wanted to say that to him when he stepped high out of the post office and jumped back into the truck after giving Liz a pat on the top of her head, but I didn't. Articulating the origins of our affections to someone are often too awkward to do, so we keep quiet.

There is an elegance about Tanya that is especially noticeable because she is so very no-nonsense. She always carries a keen intelligence about her and she does not suffer fools, yet kindness shines out of her face.

We leave the post office and Wendell drives slowly through Port Royal—immortalized as Port William in his novels—and looks mournfully on some of the empty storefronts. "Way back, on a Saturday night, there would be so many people downtown you couldn't stir them with a stick," he says. He shows me the house where his mother grew up, the farm his ancestors worked, and the Baptist church his grandfather cofounded. He tells me with delight that his grandfather was dissatisfied with how close the builders were planning to plant the church to the road so he waited until after dark and moved the stakes so it'd be situated more to his liking; the builders raised the building, none the wiser, and it stands there still today. Beyond the church is a kempt graveyard. "My people are all buried there," he says.

Back at home, Tanya has made lunch (in our trio's parlance, it is dinner), like she does every day. "We eat together three times a day," she says as she sets out the food. "That's important, I think." There is meatloaf ("Leftover from last night," she says to me, with a brief smile), coleslaw, new potatoes, and a sliced tomato. There is an elegance about Tanya that is especially noticeable because she is so very no-nonsense. She always carries a keen intelligence about her and she does not suffer fools, yet kindness shines out of her face. No one would ever guess she's in her early eighties—her face does not betray this, nor does her dexterity in her kitchen. Her first book, a folio of photographs called *For the Hog Killing, 1979*, will be published soon, but she is too modest to talk about it. When I ask about the exact release date, she shrugs. "Oh, I don't know a thing about that," she says.

For anyone who knows him, it is clear that there is no Wendell without Tanya. He rarely says the word "I" without preceding it with the phrase "Tanya and." Sitting together at the eating table, they are like two parts on the same machine, finishing one another's sentences, complementing each other's stories. Occasionally Wendell misses a word or two because of poor hearing, and Tanya yells out to him to clarify. They are partners, and seeing them together helps me to strengthen my own marriage. It is hard to be in the presence of these two and not feel like you are always learning something.

Similarly, it's difficult not to hang on every word that Wendell says, eager to catch the wisdom in every sentence. But it is important for us not to make Wendell into a saint. He would not like that. And he's not a saint. He's a real human being, with joys and sorrows, with attributes and faults, some of which have been on display while he's onstage or in his writing. Only a complicated person could create poetry, essays, and fiction that speak so soundly to the human experience and resonate so firmly with so many of us.

Our dinner conversation is about the sad news of the world, friends we have in common, and books. Tanya is a voracious reader, especially of novels, and tells me about her recent favorites. Wendell, who has long loved Ben Jonson, is reading him again, and is particularly taken with the tale

of Jonson's walk from London to Edinburgh. Our talk is one of laughter and sadness. Often the laughter comes at points in discussing the modern political atmosphere when the only other sensible reaction would be to cry. Wendell has lost patience with all sides of the argument, both liberal and conservative, and fears that constructive conversation has come to a halt not only in the halls of Congress but also in living rooms, beauty salons, and front porches. But here we are, three people, who, despite having much in common, also have many differences and are busy in discussion pocked mostly with affection for one another and for our country. "Obviously there is some risk in making affection the pivot of an argument about economy," Wendell started his 2012 Jefferson Lecture. It seems to me that joy, sorrow, and affection are the three things always present in a conversation with him.

There are strawberries, pound cake, and custard for dessert. We savor the taste of summer together.

Out on the porch a nice breeze rises off the Kentucky River and washes over us as we visit together. The little house sits only a hundred steps from the river, Wendell tells me, and obviously he takes great pleasure in this. As we look out from our perch, Wendell tells me the history of this spot of land that was once the major waterfront for Port Royal. There is an old store just down the hill that is now used for storage, and Wendell knows the exact date that it closed, the name of the man who ran it, and stories of the people who used to congregate there. Liz stands nearby, tail flapping easily, her eyes latched on his face as he talks, waiting for his attention to fall upon her. Wendell moves across the porch and squats down to put his hand out toward another border collie who has been hiding under a wicker chair. Her name is Maggie, and she is obviously much older, with a whitened muzzle and a humble, bent composure. She touches her tongue to his hand and props her head back atop her paws. Wendell looks around to me with sorrow on his eyes. "Maggie is an old dog now," he says.

When I leave, Wendell and Tanya perform the southern tradition of standing on the porch until I have left, waving and calling out as I skip down the steps back toward my car at the foot of the hill. When I have disappeared from their view, I turn around to look back. They cannot see me, but I can see them, hidden as I am in a little copse of summertime trees. Tanya slips back into the house, but Wendell remains for a moment, his fists on his hips. He looks out toward the river, hidden from his view by the lush green trees of August. ("I go among trees and sit still," he famously wrote.) He has told me that once the leaves fall, he will be able to see the water again, from his front porch. Today he is bearing witness to the trees, and they are a gracious plenty. Once autumn comes, he will look and see the river, churning, rolling.

CRYSTAL WILKINSON

KAREN M^cELMURRAY

The day is summer-hot, the sky full of rain clouds as I park and cross the street. It's the first time I've been to Wild Fig bookstore, but the bricked steps remind me already of a house from the past I can't quite name. A John Muir quote is taped to one of the tall windows: *All that the sun shines on is beautiful, so long as it is wild.* I think of a yard with sweet peas and a voice calling to me from the front porch. The Wild Fig's porch is like where I read all summer long, dreaming of books to be written. Inside, the place is cool, and it has the scent of coffee grounds and sweets to make a mouth water.

All week, I've been reading Crystal's work. I've read *The Birds of Opulence* and *Blackberries, Blackberries,* and I have a brand-new copy of *Water Street* to fill me up at bedtime. I know Crystal from conferences and readings, and I know the amazing year she's just had. The Ernest J. Gaines Award for Literary Excellence. The Judy Young Gaines Prize for Fiction. The Weatherford Award for Appalachian Fiction. Appalachian Book of the Year from the Appalachian Writer's Association. I've filled my notepad with questions about the life that took her toward these awards. *The women you write. How much are they based on you? Talk to me about making art in a hard world.* I have spoken to Crystal a couple of times on the phone, and I am hoping that today's conversation will be as real as her soft, rich voice. A conversation, a real getting-to-know.

Crystal sits comfortably on a leather sofa in the front room of Wild Fig, her laptop open. For all I know she could at that very moment be conjuring the lush prose I've been loving all week. She has, she says, just a few messages to check, and so I walk the rooms of the bookstore, coveting books from a shelf where a note from Bayard Rustin reads, "We need, in every community, a group of angelic troublemakers." I order tea and a strawberry tart and finally settle in on the other end of the leather couch, listening in on a nearby conversation between two young women about a writing workshop they're coteaching.

What I've found in about five minutes in Wild Fig is a community. There are events coming up—readings and signings—but it's the people who make community in this bookstore. Not that I am surprised. I've been sitting with people and communities all the while I've been reading Crystal's work. This past week I've met her characters. Lucy, dreaming as thunder rattles the windows, dreaming of the feel of every living thing on her skin, dreaming herself somewhere else, closer to the moon. I've met Yolanda who, not yet born, already gathers stories as she rubs inside the swell of her mother's belly. And I've met Joe Brown, who closes *The Birds of Opulence* by knowing deep down that it is women who have held the world up. Crystal Wilkinson's characters and places, homes left and homes longed for, are the stuff of the both ordinary and extraordinary lives of her writing. As we take a seat at a quiet table by a window and begin talking, intimate time flies down and settles between us like a small, comfortable critter.

> *Crystal Wilkinson's characters and places, homes left and homes longed for, are the stuff of the both ordinary and extraordinary lives of her writing.*

Homecoming and home-leaving, I say to Crystal, feeling my way toward the heartwood I've found these last days as I've read her work. *Heartwood.* The center. The breath of life I've felt rise from her pages, ready for this day of talking. What I feel in your work, I say, is the simultaneous longing for and loss of home. The wish, always, to get back to the place that made us—all the while we know deep in ourselves that those rooms and places and times are long gone. Yes, she says. *The where we were and where we are now.* And from there it is almost effortless, the way we move from questions about longing to questions about the world that made us as women writers.

How do we make the invisible visible? It's the question, one with which I am very familiar. How, as a woman from Appalachia, do we not only find our voices, but make ourselves heard? We recognize each other right away around this question for women artists, but Crystal's experience goes deeper than being invisible as a woman and struggling to find that *here I am*. As a writer, hers is an intergenerational story. As she says, she writes as a human being from rural Appalachia and a Black human being. Issues of gender, sexism, sexual trauma, race, and racism compound the essential question of why and how we write. What does it mean to be from a Black rural family in Appalachia and find the stories for that experience? As W. E. B. Du Bois said so well, Crystal's coming-to-voice is not only a story of silence and language, but one of the triple consciousness of being a Black American, a rural American, and a woman.

And then there's being the crazy woman's daughter, a story we share right away. My own mother suffered from a mental illness the family never claimed, though it had the shape of OCD, the taste of schizophrenia, an echo of abuse that will be forever unnamed. I feel it deep inside, Crystal's story of her mother. Ever since she was seventeen, she says, she has been holding herself up to the light, holding her mother up to that same light. *Is this what I am becoming? Who are we when both love and madness are part of our heritage?* Crystal saw her mother, Dorsie, hospitalized literally hundreds of times and as a result was raised by her granny. At a distance, she knew a mother who was medicated, lost—and also a mother who was the possessor of a desperate, controlling love. As Crystal spoke of Dorsie, that voice I'd heard on the phone came back to me in all its tenderness and sorrow. Love and madness were both part of Crystal's inheritance from family, and that inheritance came down to her as questions. *How do we single out one thread from the fabric of our pasts and follow it back to our own hearts? Can that thread of both love and loss find its way to the writing?*

Ten years ago, Crystal Wilkinson became brave enough to write about Dorsie, and in that writing, she did not see her mother as a darkness. Having given herself permission to write her mother's story, the words began to lead to an understanding of love that had not been spoken, and of a mental illness that had possessed lives. That writing, of course, has not been easy. Crystal describes this work as a descent into a womb of grief, a well of pain and anger that she must write from in order to become new again, especially since the work has coincided with Dorsie's recent death. As she

wrote during a recent writing retreat: "Solitude with my own thoughts and words is satisfying and restorative and terrifying. And the water here. I'm so drawn to it, and still so afraid of it. I almost drowned when I was a child, and that has always been a baseline of fear. I am drawn to being on the lake and embracing my fears and turning them inside out, and being on all that water, though I don't know how to swim, gives me a peace that I can't explain."

Writing from pain has meant breaking from the past both personally and aesthetically. Crystal has had to ask herself whether a new self, and her new work, needs new forms. Does fiction most suit hurt and anger, abandonment and love, or is fiction a mask to hide behind? Is memoir the best vehicle for this story? How many times will she have to begin again to arrive at the heart of this story? At this writing, she plans a January sabbatical—a much-needed break from her teaching life—to focus on the story of her mother and herself.

By this point we've been talking for almost two hours, and my cup of tea has to be refilled. We walk around the Wild Fig, looking for a place to charge my ailing cell phone, and we fall into conversation with the two young women who are leading writing workshops. We talk for a bit with Ronald Davis, Crystal's partner, and we both breathe deep. We're transitioning from talking about the bodies of dark water that one must cross to reach our truths. And I have so many other questions for Crystal. I want to know about her choice of a fragmented, lyric voice for her novels. I want to know about work that has influenced her in terms of style. So we talk for a while about Jean Toomer. We talk about Susan Minot and Gloria Naylor and Louise Erdrich. By then we're seated again in our Wild Fig nook, the little table by the window overlooking the street. I'm thinking about how Crystal's soothing voice is like a quilt pattern. Like a quilt piece that is a star or a cabin window, her voice falls naturally next to my own, and we talk like girls sharing our secrets. Like this, she begins to talk with me about rooms.

From that small room she could hear voices from the rest of the house, and thus began a passing-down, room unto room, small nesting places, holy places, where there was a sense of history, of all the times before.

The first place she remembers writing is upstairs, a room in her granny's house. Like memory, that room connects to time upon time. The room belonged to her grandmother before her, and it was also her mother's before that. From that small room she could hear voices from the rest of the house, and thus began a passing-down, room unto room, small nesting places, holy places, where there was a sense of history, of all the times before. We talk about her writing days at the recent retreat in western Kentucky. We talk about a writing retreat sponsored by the Kentucky Foundation for Women that she attended. We talk about a room at the Mary Anderson Center—a rustic dorm room with pale morning light and moonlight enough to light up the words on the page. Like love passed from generation to generation, room passes into room in our conversation. I tell her about a room upstairs, also at a granny's house, with the sound of rain on a tin roof, the generations of ghosts in an attic. I tell her about a retreat of my own in a town

called Eureka Springs, a room in a house off a gravel road, how time passed without clocks there. And just like that, I'm back where this morning of conversation began—my wish for our voices to converge, my wish to find a center that is as rich and real as the pages of Crystal's beautiful writing.

And suddenly there we are, at the end of our talking time. There we are with our shared history of writing spaces, our shared history of both grief and finding the salvation of writing. "I haven't been to church in years," Crystal says, "but I do believe in a higher power. I sound like my granny back in that house where I grew up, but I do believe God's in control." God, I think, as I finish my third cup of tea, as I hug Crystal's neck one more time and head out into the streets of Lexington for a summer afternoon. I think God, at least for me on this day, is in the power of sharing not only space, but our voices. Words and common experience, stories so alive I can taste them. As I get in my car and begin to drive away the last words of *Birds of Opulence* come to me again: "a hundred tongues whispering home, home, home."

NOTE: *On that summer day in 2018 when I visited the Wild Fig, it was owned by Crystal Wilkinson and Ronald Davis. Today the Wild Fig is a cooperative, a majority Black-owned bookstore and a safe space to build community.*

RON RASH

WILEY CASH

I almost always start with an image," Ron Rash has said. "I never outline, I never plot. I just see where the image will take me."

Since his earliest published books—the story collection *The Night the New Jesus Fell to Earth and Other Stories from Cliffside, North Carolina* (1994), the poetry collection *Eureka Mill* (1998), and the novel *One Foot in Eden* (2002)—the images Ron Rash has offered readers have been numerous and haunting. In his novel *Serena*, a powerful woman rides horseback across a ridge, an eagle perched on her arm. In the short story "The Ascent," a young boy escapes his meth-ravaged home and finds solace in a crashed airplane, the dead pilot and passenger still inside. In the poem "Three AM and the Stars Were Out," a ringing telephone stirs an old veterinarian from sleep, and he sets out in the dead of night to doctor whatever farm animal awaits him.

Aside from their resonance, these images also serve Rash's readers by illuminating Appalachia and the people who live there. Rash is an ethnographer of the region's heart, a heart that is plumbed in stories like "Last Rites," in which a woman begins an impossible journey to find the body of her murdered son, and poems like "The Search," in which a group of white farmers spend a frigid night in the woods, looking for an elderly African-American woman who has wandered away from home. He is also a chronicler of a place that is and has always been in transition. In Rash's work, natives of Appalachia discover Native American artifacts in turned fields. Log cabin settlers who rely on the barter economy help raise grandchildren who will make their living from state-sanctioned tobacco allotments. As elderly adults these same tobacco farmers will pause in their fieldwork and watch outsiders stream into the mountains, and they will either mourn or celebrate as resorts and expensive homes spring up on the land that surrounds them.

Eudora Welty said, "One place understood helps us understand all places better." I agree with her, and I know that Rash, who is a founding member of Narrative 4, an international organization that bridges cultural divides through story exchanges, would agree with her too. Welty and other Mississippi writers like William Faulkner and Walker Percy were writers from a state that wanted to be understood, a state that so often felt like it stood apart from the rest of the country for reasons both good and bad. It was Mississippi against the world, and that kind of tension makes for great stories, and has led to great stories in which Mississippi explains itself to the rest of us.

Rash was eight years old when the family returned to western North Carolina and the landscape that his ancestors had called home since the eighteenth century.

But North Carolina is not Mississippi. It is not a place that looks across state lines for slights and affronts both real and imagined. No, North Carolina is a state with a long history of confronting itself, and nowhere are these confrontations more apparent than the state's mountains. It could be argued that story is born of tension, and this is true of Rash's fiction. For example, in his novel *Above the Waterfall* a community is divided when an elderly local is accused of poisoning a resort's trout stream, and in his short story "Lincolnites," a young widow exacts revenge against a Confederate soldier. Even his poetry, which almost always traces a narrative thread, is driven by confrontation. Such is the case in "Flying Squadron," a poem about union members who face violence while trying to organize workers in textile mills.

But in Rash's work these wars are not always interpersonal. Communities fight environmental change wrought by industrial destruction. Lives are devastated by addiction and prescription drugs. The rugged terrain of the Appalachian Mountains has historically served to preserve folkways, but if the good stays in then the bad does too, and if you do not live there, you may not see it. But Ron Rash and the international reputation he has garnered makes certain that life in Appalachia is felt and understood beyond the rim of the hills.

Rash has said that "landscape is destiny," and it certainly seems so in his life. Born in Chester, South Carolina, to a mother and father who left the mountains for work in the textile mills, Rash was eight years old when the family returned to western North Carolina and the landscape that his ancestors had called home since the eighteenth century. He completed college

at Gardner-Webb University in Boiling Springs, North Carolina, and received a master's degree from Clemson University in South Carolina. He got married, took a job teaching at Tri-County Community College in Murphy, North Carolina, welcomed a daughter and a son, and threw himself into writing about Appalachia with an intensity and dedication that has not yielded after nearly three decades. He has achieved a level of popular success and critical acclaim that is uncommon, especially for literary writers who are too often dismissed simply as being regional authors. A *New York Times* best-selling author, he has won an O. Henry Award, the Frank O'Connor International Short Story Award, a grant from the National Endowment for the Arts, and a Guggenheim Award, and he has twice been a finalist for the PEN/Faulkner Award for Fiction. He has been teaching at Western Carolina University since 2003, and he currently serves as the

John A. Parris Jr. and Dorothy Luxton Parris Distinguished Professor of Appalachian Cultural Studies.

These accomplishments are impressive for any writer, especially a writer born of textile mills and tobacco fields, a writer whose earliest impressions of the power of story came at the hands of a grandfather who used his wit to hide his own illiteracy while "reading" to his grandson. Even though he was a child, it did not take Rash long to understand that his grandfather used pictures in books as cues to make up stories. Every time his grandfather read the same book, the story changed, and Rash was mesmerized with the alterations in plot, dialogue, and characterization.

If landscape is destiny, then what will come of the Appalachian landscape about which Ron Rash writes? It is not as easy to change the arc of history as it is to change the story in a picture book. There are only so

many trees to cut down before there are no trees left. There are only so many streams to poison before no clean water remains. And there are only so many mountains to remove before there are no mountains standing. The land and its people are shifting and adapting to changes in climate, culture, and civic life, and Rash has spent decades chronicling the region's evolution. Rash has called Appalachia "a landscape I cannot exhaust," but unlike the tools of the industrialists and developers who enter the mountains, plunder them, and leave, Rash uses the tools of the writer to record what he sees and what he knows to be true. His literary mining of Appalachia is regenerative and restorative; it holds the mirror of the past up to the present moment and shows us what the region was, what it is, and what it could be.

ADRIANA TRIGIANI

AMY D. CLARK

I live in Big Stone Gap, Virginia, two houses down from the stately, nineteenth-century home where Adriana Trigiani grew up. I pass the house every day as I walk my dog around the block, imagining a budding young writer hard at work at her desk in the late 1960s and early 1970s as she waits for the Wise County bookmobile to arrive.

Born to a big Italian family, she left Big Stone Gap at age eighteen and now lives in New York City. As of this publication, she has written twelve novels (both adult and YA) and contributed to several anthologies; she has written for television, film, and stage; she has written and directed movies; she launched a travel and cosmetics business; and she cofounded a non-profit program that serves thousands of young writers in Virginia.

The more notable of her works set in Appalachia is the Big Stone Gap trilogy, inspired by Adriana's hometown in far southwest Virginia. Her 1970s characters resist Appalachian archetypes: the narrator is a strong, professional woman of Italian heritage surrounded by empathetic men. And while her books may include themes that appeal to wide audiences (such as romance and searching for long-lost family), her protagonist, as she has said in interviews, grapples with what it means to feel like an outsider in her own community, much like she did as a child. "My novel is there to provide a bridge to your own fertile imagination and dreams," Adriana told me. "I learned this walk growing up in Big Stone Gap, Virginia, listening to riveting stories as they were told."

In today's Appalachia, the concept of identity and the discussion surrounding it has finally cracked traditional definitions of what it means to be Appalachian. What does it mean to be Catholic or Jewish in a predominantly Protestant community, for example? What does it mean to be gay in Appalachia? Black or Latina in Appalachia? What does it mean to fight for the environment in Appalachia when you come from a family of coal miners?

As writers and authors, their backgrounds and approaches to the craft of writing might be different, but somehow, their storytelling, and the essence of the truth and how they seek it, is Appalachian.

These are the very questions that kids are answering in the writing they do in The Origin Project (TOP). Adriana has used her influence and inspiration, nurtured by her own upbringing, to encourage kids to write about their communities and identities in this nonprofit writing program she co-founded with Executive Director Nancy Bolmeier Fisher. The project began in far southwest Virginia and was embedded in the public school curriculum; it has since expanded toward northern Virginia with more than a thousand students who write from personal experience and interviews with family and community members. Students also benefit from workshops with well-known writers Adriana introduces to them, including Margo Lee Shetterly, Meg Wolitzer, and Laurie Eustis. TOP has published four volumes of student work about their communities, families, and identities, in which they write about struggle, nostalgia, and everything in between. "As writers and authors, their backgrounds and approaches to the craft of writing might be different, but somehow, their storytelling, and the essence of the truth and how they seek it, is Appalachian," Trigiani says. "That's what we strive to bring the students. That's our hope."

But it might be the movie she made in Big Stone Gap that will be her lasting love letter to her Appalachian town. For over a decade, she passed up opportunities to make the movie in places that were more convenient, less expensive, and outside the United States. The movie, she said, belonged

to the people of Big Stone Gap. She wanted the people of her town, people she'd grown up with, to be immortalized on-screen.

She had a role for everyone, even me. A year before, I had published a book about the many ways we speak English in the Appalachian region. Before she began filming, Trigiani called me, asking me if I'd consider reading the script and do a kind of "phonetic rendering" of some of the words in case the actors needed a bit of reminding on how to say things like "married," as if they had grown up in central Appalachia.

She made all of us feel as if we were necessary to this movie becoming what she envisioned. It was as much about the place as the story.

We cried to see Mutual Drug, which had closed its doors for good just a

year before, reopened and stocked just as it would have been in the 1970s. To see our main street featured just the way it is—the Southwest Virginia Museum, the landscape we drive through on the way to work every morning—all immortalized on-screen. The community answered casting calls to film wedding scenes, the outdoor drama scenes, Christmas decorating in the museum. Those famous actors lived among us, shopped in our market, spent time in the local bookstore.

And when we watched the movie for the first time, we pointed, smiled, and laughed to see ourselves. We shared it with people we loved. We sat in the dark through all the credits, just to see names from our town on the screen.

> *And when we watched the movie for the first time,*
> *we pointed, smiled, and laughed to see ourselves.*
> *We shared it with people we loved.*

Then, Adriana did something else. She held a red-carpet event for the town. The actors came back and celebrated with us, took selfies with us, and smiled with us in streets that had not been that full since the 1940s.

It's quiet again in Big Stone Gap, but every now and then some tourists will come through because of her books or the movie. The set of Carmine's is now a shiny visitor's center where we hold block parties, movie nights, jam sessions. She did something that most authors whose places are based on their beloved hometowns probably dream of being able to do. The novel is a solitary act of creation, as is reading. But the novel as film brought us together in a different way that may keep us bound together for generations.

Adriana's home community is rural, a common setting in literature about Appalachia. Rural living is often associated with the problems that drive literary plots. But her stories are also set in New York City, in the Italian Alps, in the golden age of Hollywood. Her characters are rural townspeople and villagers, but they're also businesspeople, celebrities, and middle-class workers. What binds them together is that working people are at the core of the story, she says, because she comes from working people who understand the tension between leaving and staying. In Adriana's words:

The truth of mountain people everywhere on Planet Earth is that they
speak from experience, as my people in Italy are for the most part,
from the mountains, having thrived in small villages in the Alps for
generations. It was not chance that our Italian-American family found
ourselves in Big Stone Gap. Now, my cousins, my age and younger, have
left the mountains in Italy to make a living, just as I did when the time
came. If you talk to anyone in Appalachia, many of their children leave
to have experiences elsewhere. Some return to live, and some don't,
either by necessity or choice. This is always a tussle of a conversation
when I'm home. A sort of lightweight us and them conversation about
who leaves and stays, as if choosing one or the other determines your
level of love and devotion to the place and its people. I offer this instead:
once you have the Appalachian experience, honey, you are one. Perhaps
this is the best definition of "modern" Appalachia.

When I think of modern Appalachia, I am guided by writers who explore its complexity in resistance to the singular image people have long held about the place and its people. By complexity, I mean we are looking beyond beliefs about Appalachia and its people, particularly stereotypical beliefs about race, gender, sexuality, religion, and class. Artists—writers, filmmakers, musicians, and the like—are critical in helping to reshape and expand this singular perception. Adriana Trigiani is one of those.

What comes to mind when Adriana Trigiani thinks of modern Appalachia?

She thinks of those same writers like "the queen, Barbara Kingsolver; the steady river, Silas House; and the drum majorette of the modern voice of these hills, Lee Smith," along with Amy Greene, Wiley Cash, and poet Nikki Giovanni. Roanoker Beth Macy's *Dopesick*, she says, "should be required reading for every American." Appalachia's narratives have "taken root," she says, "because the nuances of the cultural life, language, and history of the Appalachians are being written about in the context of the roots of the American experience."

Writers like these empower us with choices beyond the influences of our upbringing and everything else that shapes how we think about what it means to be Appalachian, or to be in today's Appalachia.

Beyond all that is the story. And Adriana Trigiani is a master storyteller.

SILAS HOUSE

AMY GREENE

One night I sat with my friend on a porch in a hollow, looking up at the stars through the close trees. He was smoking, but that was a secret. He had kicked the habit over ten years back. We were in the dark woods of eastern Kentucky, at Hindman Settlement School. We had been there for a week, talking with like-minded others about writing, the thing we both love and have loved since childhood. At the moment, though, we weren't talking about anything. We were just being still together in the mountains we have also both loved, as much as the writing, since childhood.

My friend was Silas House. Before he was my friend, he was the writer I admired most. I didn't learn about his work until I went back to school in my late twenties, as an adult college student studying in the Green Mountains of Vermont. A thousand miles away from my own Smoky Mountains for the first time, I immersed myself in Appalachian literature. Somehow, it took getting away from home to better understand home. I learned what it meant to be Appalachian by leaving Appalachia. I learned what it meant to write Appalachian by reading Silas House.

As a child growing up on a farm in rural East Tennessee, there was plenty of Appalachian folklore on our grade-school reading lists. In our libraries there were Jack Tales at storytime. At my house we had a *Reader's Digest* condensed version of Catherine Marshall's historical classic *Christy*, its spine broken and its yellowed pages dog-eared. After I got married at

eighteen and left home, I read Lee Smith's *Oral History*, a revelation of sorts to me as an aspiring writer in its reverent depiction of our geography and its authentic rendering of our dialect. But I hadn't been exposed to books about contemporary Appalachia that reflected my own perception of my place.

When I read the opening pages of Silas House's debut novel *Clay's Quilt*, in which a four-year-old boy rides toward a bloody murder over an icy mountain during a snowstorm with his mother and a man who is not his father, a stillness stole into me, not unlike the one I experienced a decade later sitting with my friend on a porch in a dark Kentucky hollow. I was in a place that I knew, in the hands of an author that I already trusted. I recognized the landscape he described, the words his characters spoke, the way of life he portrayed. This writer was telling the truth.

Once I finished *Clay's Quilt*, I set about reading Silas House's entire body of work. Alongside stage plays and works of nonfiction, House has written *Clay's Quilt* and five other novels, *A Parchment of Leaves* (2001), *The Coal*

Tattoo (2004), *Eli the Good* (2009), *Same Sun Here* (2012), and *Southernmost* (2018). They all give me the same feeling of being told the whole truth about a region of the country that has been by turns romanticized and vilified by those unborn to it. The first piece of advice House gave me, not long after we met at Lincoln Memorial University where he was then writer-in-residence and where I had come to read in the chapel from my own debut novel, was this: "Don't just write what you know. Write what you know to be true."

Silas House and I know many of the same things to be true. We were raised by the same working-class people. We both encountered the wider world through pop culture, watching the same movies and television shows, listening to the same music. We went to the same Pentecostal churches. We waded in the same creeks and lay under the same beech trees. We have both felt compelled for complicated reasons to share in writing our complicated love of the same home.

But Silas House's love of his native Appalachia has manifested far beyond the pages of his books. As much as he is a writer, he is a humanitarian. In 2011, along with Wendell Berry, House launched a sit-in at Kentucky Governor Steve Beshear's office to protest mountaintop removal mining. In his efforts to protect his mountains, he has marched on his state capitol in Frankfort, Kentucky, and on his nation's capitol in Washington, D.C. As an extension of his activism, House has taught undergraduate students at Berea College. He serves as the faculty advisor for Berea's Harvey Milk Society, a student group that organizes protests and marches for LGBTQ+ rights. As a professor, he has taken his students out into the streets with him, urging them to strive for political change. He has taught them both to write and to care. He has taught me the same things.

As an extension of his activism, House has taught undergraduate students at Berea College. He serves as the faculty advisor for Berea's Harvey Milk Society, a student group that organizes protests and marches for LGBTQ+ rights.

Since discovering *Clay's Quilt* years ago in the Green Mountains of Vermont, I have seen the home I've always known through different eyes. Since meeting Silas House, I have taken the advice he gave me, to write not just what I know, but what I know to be true. I write about the struggles of Appalachian people, which are not unlike the struggles of people anywhere else. I write about the beauty and brutality of the Appalachian landscape. I try to convey in words what matters about this place that has been deemed by the rest of the country not to matter. I write about the promise, as Berry says in his poem "A Vision," that can be found in our hardship, which is so not only for us but for other regions of America where cycles of poverty and violence have been hard to break. I try to tell the world beyond the mountains, as House has done through his books and his activism, that if you pay attention to us, and you don't discount us, you might see by watching us rise what hope is possible for and inherent in all of humanity.

In *Clay's Quilt*, and in Silas House's other novels, there is bloodshed and music, there are dark hollows and grassy wildflower balds. Sitting on the porch with my friend, sharing a forbidden cigarette, the air was smoky and sweet with mountain laurel, both at once. We didn't have to say anything out loud. We just knew what was true. We were still. We were safe. We were home.

GEORGE ELLA LYON

PATRICIA HUDSON

On a sweltering summer evening in 1983, George Ella Lyon stood up to read her poetry at the Appalachian Writer's Workshop at the Hindman Settlement School in eastern Kentucky. The youngest member of the workshop's faculty, George Ella had just published her first poetry chapbook titled *Mountain*. The buildings at the Settlement School weren't air-conditioned, and the day had been so steamy that the podium had been pulled outside and set up on the front porch. Cicadas thrummed in the trees as the audience arranged folding chairs in ragged rows on the driveway, fanning themselves and praying for a breeze.

I was a twenty-something journalist, an Appalachian native, attending my first literary workshop. I'd found a place to sit at the edge of the crowd, feeling out of place, unsure what to expect. All I knew about George Ella was that she was a poet and that she looked to be about my age. Up to that point, my exposure to poetry had been confined to the dead-white-male poets I'd encountered in my college textbooks, and most of their work hadn't resonated with me. I'd arrived at the workshop believing I had a poetic tin ear, but on that twilight evening, as George Ella began to read, her voice carried across the lawn and I felt something shift. It was the first time I'd heard poetry about my place, my Appalachia.

In the midst of reading her poem "Salvation," George Ella broke into song—two lines from the folk ballad "Pretty Saro"—weaving a melody from

the region's past into her present-day poem, offering her listeners both roots and wings. And then suddenly, there were literal wings among us as a bird darted through the crowd, flew past George Ella, and smacked hard into a window. It dropped into the bushes amid a startled silence. After a few seconds, George Ella resumed reading, though she glanced over her shoulder from time to time, hoping to see the bird rise, phoenix-like, from the shrubbery.

At the end of the reading, as the crowd dispersed, I pushed my way into the bushes looking for the bird, only to meet George Ella approaching from the other side. What we found in the dust beneath the window was a sparrow, the commonest of birds, ruffled and brown and definitely dead. We carried its limp remains down to Troublesome Creek, the meandering stream that flows through the Settlement School's campus, and buried it on the bank in unspoken agreement that this tiny, feathered life deserved some small measure of respect. Our friendship grew from the bones of that bird.

I came away from that night with three important things: a newfound love of poetry, the thrill of finding a writing community of fellow Appalachians, and the seeds of a lifelong friendship.

Fast-forward more than thirty years: George Ella has now published nearly fifty books, everything from poetry collections to novels to picture books. She was named Kentucky's Poet Laureate for 2015–16 and has won numerous other regional and national awards, including the American Library Association's Schneider Family Book Award, Appalachian Book of the Year, and Golden Kite Award. Yet nearly every summer she returns to the banks of Troublesome Creek to introduce a new gathering of writers to their Appalachia, helping them launch their own journey of poetic self-discovery.

As a child growing up in Harlan, Kentucky, George Ella discovered her love of words from hearing her parents read poetry aloud, but she was also keenly aware of the stereotypes that haunt Appalachia. When her seventh-grade class went on a field trip from Harlan to the Kentucky capitol, "Our teacher told us not to talk or folks would know where we came from." Even decades later, when she recounts that story, her voice is incredulous. "Folks in Appalachia are told, over and over, that they aren't acceptable. We're told we need to change, to remake ourselves."

George Ella left the mountains after high school, earning a bachelor's degree from Centre College, an MA from the University of Arkansas, and a PhD from Indiana University. During those years, she discovered the vital connection between her poetic voice and her Appalachian roots. In an essay titled "Voiceplace," she wrote, "Where you're from is not who you are, but it's an important ingredient. I believe you must trust your first voice—the one tuned by the people and place that made you—before you can speak your deepest truths."

She returned to the region and began to write poetry that depicted mountain culture as rich and deserving of respect. She also sensed that Appalachia's children needed to see their place portrayed in books in order to believe that their own experiences mattered, so she began writing picture books that nurtured not only a love of language, but also a sense of place.

Over the years, she's made hundreds of visits to schools, sharing her love of words and helping children understand that writers aren't magical beings from somewhere "out there," but folks just like themselves who must arrange and rearrange their words countless times before they appear in print. She often shows the children a tightly rolled scroll made from dozens of drafts of one of her books. She's taped the manuscript pages end to end, so when the students unroll it, it wraps around the room several times, a paper trail of try and fail and try again, giving them permission to do the same with their own words.

[Her writing studio is] a place of contemplation, a place where words, both written and spoken, bubble up and hang in the air so that those who cross the threshold seem to breathe them in.

In 1993, George Ella wrote a poem called "Where I'm From." It began: "I am from clothespins" and went on to examine the things, large and small, that shaped her. Over the years, the poem has been used as a writing prompt in schools, prisons, and rehab facilities. During one school visit, an angry teen said, "It's none of your business where I'm from." George Ella responded, "So write about that." When the girl read her poem to the class, "her anger scorched the paper," George Ella recalls, "but I watched her feel the power of her words. She felt heard."

"Where I'm From" has unlocked memories and called forth emotions in places far beyond its Appalachian roots. "Teachers have used it in all fifty states and around the world in places like China, Norway, Croatia, Indonesia, even a refugee camp in the Sudan," George Ella says. "It's out there doing its work. I'm in awe of where it's gone."

Self-discovery remains at the heart of George Ella's work, both as a writer and a teacher. Her cozy writing studio in Lexington, Kentucky, contains her writing desk, a comfy couch, a rocking chair, musical instruments, and a Hopi prayer circle made of stones. It's a place of contemplation, a place where words, both written and spoken, bubble up and hang in the air so that those who cross the threshold seem to breathe them in.

"In the Hopi tradition, when you step into the circle, the leader says, 'I

see you,' and you respond, 'I am here.' People today don't feel seen or heard, particularly in Appalachia. That's what we, as artists, can do—help people find their voices and feel heard."

George Ella has proven, time and again, that with a bit of encouragement, even the commonest of birds can rise, phoenix-like, discover its voice, and sing.

FRANK X WALKER

DENTON LOVING

rank X Walker enters the Carnegie Center for Literacy and Learning wearing a long-sleeved blue shirt. I can't make out most of the words or the design on the shirt, but "Celebrate" is large and clear. The word complements the man's confident smile, as well as his reputation. One of our mutual friends has described him as the coolest, most charming poet in Kentucky, and it's easy to see why.

The Carnegie Center for Literacy and Learning is housed in Lexington's original public library building. When the center was first established in 1992, Walker served on its original advisory board.

"I like this space. It feels like home to me. All this is an important idea. It's a literary space," he says with visible joy at the idea of a physical location dedicated to the written word. When we speak Walker is about a month away from releasing his eleventh volume of poetry, *Last Will, Last Testament, with a public reading at the Carnegie Center.*

Most people know Walker only as a poet. I'd long known that he studied fiction with Gurney Norman as an undergraduate at the University of Kentucky, but I was surprised to learn that during those years, Walker was pulled toward visual art more than writing. Coinciding with the reading, the center will host an exhibit of his original visual art, the first time in more than thirty years that he's shown this kind of work to the public.

"I gave up visual art because I couldn't feed my kid," Walker says. "I just made the decision that our survival was the most important thing so we agreed that I would focus on something else, and that ended up being administration and writing."

To say that he found success in that choice is an understatement. He's served in administrative roles at the Martin Luther King Cultural Center at the University of Kentucky, at the Black Cultural Center at Purdue University, and he directed the Kentucky Governor's School for the Arts for eleven years.

What if during the middle passage, some of the slave ships came from outer space and captured Africans and then took them back to space and then four hundred years later brought them back?

Walker shows me images of his artwork on his cell phone. The first five pieces are from the 1990s. There are twenty-seven multimedia pieces in all, ranging from a wood carving to drawings, sketches, paintings, and assemblages of cut paper. Many of the artworks were completed the previous year, coinciding with the birth of his son, while he was on paternity leave and living outside of Washington, DC. He explains that some of the images, such as a long horizontal acrylic titled *Keeneland or Churchill Downs*, were inspired by a yearning for Kentucky: "I'm missing Kentucky if I'm painting horses and black jockeys." Some images capture his wife and their new son. Others explore Afrofuturism and the middle passage with depictions of slave ships, which he says is an old obsession. Harriet Tubman reoccurs in a number of works, though in some she is unexpectedly in outer space.

"I started to imagine this idea of what if during the middle passage, some of the slave ships came from outer space and captured Africans and then took them back to space and then four hundred years later brought them back? What would it look like on the return? I imagined what if they cloned Harriet Tubman and there was an army of her. Kind of like in *Star Wars*, but an army of Harriets doing battle against enslavement on these other planets and even in the United States and around the world."

Another striking image is a self-portrait of Walker holding his son.

"I would take my son out on the front steps every morning. It was kind

of our ritual to commune with nature because it was more urban space [in DC] than I'm used to. On one particular day, his fingers were starting to work, and he could actually hold a leaf, and he was turning it over in his hand. It was a magic moment for me. My wife came out and took the picture, and I didn't know she had taken it. And there's a poem on here that I actually had written about this moment."

Beyond the beauty of this moment with his son, the painting is memorable because it's one of several where Walker has incorporated poetry into the art. A poem beginning, "it is early morning / when his tiny hands clutch / their first leaf," climbs the concrete steps of the picture.

After chatting downstairs on the Carnegie Center's first floor, we climb the stairs to the second floor to see where the work will be displayed. The gallery space isn't large, but the light is suited to visual work. Walker says he's both excited and nervous, but "having the exhibit in the same space and at the same time as introducing the new book just feels right somehow."

I can now see that his shirt says, "Celebrate the Great Outdoors" and the words circle a buffalo, immediately reminding me of *Buffalo Dance: The Journey of York*, Walker's book that gives voice to William Clark's slave, the only black man who traveled across the continent as part of the Lewis and Clark Expedition. For years now, the buffalo has served as a totem animal for Walker, and he tells me he found the shirt in Lewiston, Idaho.

Home is supposed to be wherever we're at together. So I would say that home is where we're going to be when [our] house is finished and everybody moves here. Home has always been wherever I wake up in the proximity of loved ones.

Walker enjoys traveling and visiting other places, but something always draws him back to Kentucky. I assume this is because Kentucky is home for him, but he explains that *home* is a hard word, "because my wife and kids are in Springfield, Virginia, and when I say I'm going home and I'm leaving there, and I'm saying it to her, it feels wrong. Home is supposed to be wherever we're at together. So I would say that home is where we're going to be when [our] house is finished and everybody moves here. Home has always been wherever I wake up in the proximity of loved ones."

So maybe *home* isn't the right word, but Walker admits he's always drawn back to the Bluegrass State.

"There's something about here that I'm committed to. It's not that it's just special and it's the most comfortable place for me. I think it's harder here in some ways. But there's also so much yet unrealized. And I think there's a responsibility as an uncle and a grandparent to a generation of people who I have responsibility for, who I accept responsibility for. That part of me makes it easy for me to teach because I really enjoy what happens in the classroom, and you get mostly Kentucky kids, and I know that the kind of professor Gurney Norman was when I was coming through was life-sustaining for me. Life-sustaining and life-changing. He helped me realize what it was that I should be doing. Before that, I had no freaking idea. I was just kind of wandering, and he gave me this kind of solid thing that's really been a rudder for me."

Gurney Norman with his wife Nyoka Hawkins in their roles at Old Cove Press published Walker's first book of poems, *Affrilachia*, the book that gave a sense of belonging for so many of Appalachia's people of color. To my surprise, I learn that *Affrilachia* was supposed to be a collection of short stories. Hawkins had asked to see some of Walker's stories, and almost as an afterthought, suggested he show her some poems, too. Hawkins liked the poetry so much that she forgot about the short stories.

There's something about here that I'm committed to. It's not that it's just special and it's the most comfortable place for me. I think it's harder here in some ways. But there's also so much yet unrealized.

We leave the Carnegie Center, walking into March's bright sunlight and brisk wind, and I ask Walker to help orient me to some of the rest of Lexington. He points across Gratz Park to the administrative buildings of Transylvania University. In the opposite direction, he points to downtown and the University of Kentucky. He lives in between the two directions he's pointed out, close enough to walk to the Carnegie Center and close enough to walk or bike to the University of Kentucky campus where he teaches.

In the opposite direction, he points to Cheapside, which he tells me was the slave market outside the old courthouse where older and maimed slaves, the most undesirable, were sold for discounted prices. I'm reminded that Walker—despite his visible joyfulness and charm—lives as a witness to the history of this city, this state, and this world. As much as the present, the past constantly encompasses his thoughts, and it prompts me to ask him what he sees in the present that encourages him about the future of Appalachia and Affrilachia. Without hesitation, he speaks about the young people he met three days earlier at the Annual Appalachian Studies Association Conference, held this year in Asheville, North Carolina.

"It's those young people that give me hope. I think about being at the conference and looking through the itinerary and seeing a thing called 'Affrilachian Memories.' And then to go to the event. I have nothing to do with it, and I get there, and it's a theatrical performance by two young ladies, one white, one African American, and they weave this kind of dual history about their experience with the word and then living in the space. That just blows me away. If that's what the twenty-something-year-olds are doing, I can relax. It's them. When I look at young people that I don't know doing these kinds of things that I consider proactive, progressive, potentially life changing, I'm confident they will make a difference."

MARIE JUNALUSKA

ANNETTE SAUNOOKE CLAPSADDLE

I wasn't sure you meant *this* coffee shop. I realized we have more than one now." Marie laughs as we tuck ourselves into a booth in the back corner of Qualla Java. Though the two of us make up half the clientele, the shop is loud with the sputter of brewing coffee and rubber soles against a sweating concrete floor.

"I know. I thought the same thing."

Much has changed in Cherokee, North Carolina, since the last time Marie Junaluska and I spoke, and this is an unusual place for us to meet. I've known Marie, a fluent Cherokee speaker, educator, tribal leader, and translator, my entire life. We never meet at coffee shops. We see each other at ball games, school functions, and tribal government events. She is the mother of one of my childhood friends, and she worked for my aunt Hazel beginning when Marie was fifteen years old. Unless it is a business meeting, locals rarely meet friends in coffee shops to chat. Of course, things do change.

"What used to be here?" I ask her as we settle in. Marie was born in 1950, so I am eager to get a glimpse into the world my parents' generation knew. "Like when you were growing up. What did it look like?"

"There has always been a bridge here. Yes. Always a bridge."

As she continues to piece together her memory of the place, we realize that what was once a part of her childhood life is now underground, blacktopped over—a concealed Cherokee we never think about. Tunnels, perhaps—like the ones on shows like *Unearthed*. We enjoy the mystery of it, but I can't help but lament knowing I will never see it and wondering if we can ever access it again.

This is Marie's role, though. As a translator, she makes visible the invisible. She connects memory to a new reality. She is motivated by her own desire to see and know more.

Marie has been speaking Cherokee her entire life. Her mother spoke nothing but Cherokee to her and her siblings.

Marie has been speaking Cherokee her entire life. Her mother spoke nothing but Cherokee to her and her siblings. That is not to say that she has been a student of the language in the way we prepare our current generation to be. She grew up immersed in oral Cherokee. Written Cherokee, the syllabic system developed by Sequoyah by the 1820s, was not accessible to her as a child. I assume I know the reason. Other than the Bible, books in area homes were not typical when Marie was growing up, regardless of whether it was a Cherokee home or not. I, as is often the case, am wrong about that reason, though. Marie clarifies, "When the Cherokee capital was moved from New Echota to Red Clay, the printing press was destroyed by the Georgia Guard. Everything was destroyed. I think material stopped being printed at that time. I think the material available at that time was put on a shelf. . . . Those that knew how to speak it taught us. Then as far as the schools here, we were not teaching it at all until the 1970s."

I have heard most of my life that Cherokee language was nearly eradicated because of boarding schools and often forget the impact of other federal assimilation policies and practices. An act so simple as the burning of a printing press over a hundred years ago still influences language education today. The language only survives because of people like Marie and her family. Language was, and largely still is, carried in the minds and mouths of Cherokee people and rarely in the books and papers of dusty archives. It has to *live*, to survive. People like Marie give it the heartbeat to do so.

Marie's mother only taught her two characters of the syllabary—the

characters for Jesus: tsi sa. Those two characters continue to fascinate her, as if there is a key to a secret door; the language, fully realized, is that key.

While attending day school in Wolftown, North Carolina, Marie was taught by her only Cherokee teacher, Oscar Welch, in the fifth grade. For the remainder of her formal education, Marie doesn't recall having another

Cherokee instructor. It's not a fact that seems odd to her. "I never really thought of it," she tells me. As the only Cherokee faculty member on staff at my local high school, it is something that troubles me, though. I am concerned more by how few Cherokee language teachers we have in our community who have both the skills of language proficiency and teaching methods. These are rare individuals.

Like many of her peers, Marie left home after eighth grade and attended Riverside Boarding School in Oklahoma. Stories of boarding schools in Indian Country range from transformative to tragic. For Marie, Riverside emboldened her commitment to language and culture. Ironically, being farther from home gave her perspective to appreciate the uniqueness of Cherokee culture and her gift of language. She could speak with other Cherokees and instantly return home or share her distinctive gift and discover an allusive appreciation from strangers. I watch her smile as she recounts her days at Riverside. Her memories call her attention back, and her face seems to grow more youthful in the retelling. She knows I understand what it is like to go away in order to discover home.

At Riverside she also recognized her role in a larger Native community. "It made me so proud that I could speak our language and I could hear the others speak their language. I thought, wow, we have our own too, and so we would proudly speak it," she recalls. "It's what really opened me up to our culture, our customs. Taking me away from here and seeing. Today, I am so thankful. It was a very meaningful . . . just a rewarding experience for me to go away from here . . . and get to know all these other Natives from different states. . . . Otherwise, I would have kept thinking we were the only Indians out here."

When Marie returned to North Carolina, she knew she wanted to be a teacher. Marie's Oklahoma experience exposed her to new possibilities to put both her knowledge and her approach to teaching to use. Cherokee Central Schools received a grant to teach the language, and Marie applied to work with the program, primarily because it gave her the opportunity to both teach the language and learn the syllabary in the process. "It was typical that most people did not have experience with the syllabary. I think it's been dormant," she recalls. Through this teaching opportunity, she could pursue the key she had only glimpsed as a child in those two syllabary characters her mother taught her. "I had no idea how to read and write," she remembers. "But I was ready. I was excited."

Marie is soft-spoken. I have never heard her raise her voice. I am quite sure I have never seen her frown. She is reflective and kind as she talks.

As I sit across from Marie, I already know the timeline of her career. Marie was a Cherokee Tribal Council member for most of my life, so I try to imagine her as a young teacher and it is hard for me to visualize how one makes the jump into a political life. Cherokee politics are notoriously contentious. Marie is soft-spoken. I have never heard her raise her voice. I am quite sure I have never seen her frown. She is reflective and kind as she talks. Mind you, not in that stereotypical wise-sage way that is likely expected by the tourists sipping lattes in the next booth over. We joke about her encounters with other tribes while in Oklahoma and politics in

Cherokee, but she is never mean-spirited. Her gentle demeanor comes from a place of wisdom and insight, not indifference or witlessness.

"I was pregnant when your grandmother, serving on council at the time, came to me and asked if I would work as the interpreter for tribal council. It kind of floored me. It was kind of scary. But I thought maybe I could do it because I could speak." Two months after giving birth to her first child, Marie began her career as an official interpreter for the Eastern Band of Cherokee Indians. She worked with mentors such as Beloved Woman Maggie Wachacha, whom she calls "jolly," and quickly learned the art of translating English legal documents to the Cherokee syllabary. Her work is one of sovereignty. As legal professionals do, Marie interprets law and its intent—and that is just the first step. She is the bridge between our wishes to self-govern and nation-build, and the implementation of these wishes.

"Why did you decide to run for council?" I am always fascinated by this question. Marie is a council member who served prior to and after the gaming industry came to the Eastern Band. Therefore, she has seen incredible transitions and, perhaps, motivations of our people.

It was the peoples' thought. Not mine. I never even thought about running or being a council member. One day I was in Painttown for a Community Club meeting and I thought, well here I am.

"It was the peoples' thought. Not mine. I never even thought about running or being a council member. One day I was in Painttown for a Community Club meeting and I thought, well here I am. I am living here and have kids. I should be down there and see what's going on. I just started attending sessions, and the next thing I know, they asked me if I would consider running for council. And I thought, *Oh, No! No!*" We laugh together. "I immediately said no and that person asked me again. And I said maybe the next term. But the next term didn't happen. They went ahead and put my name down."

And this is where my age shows. Marie is telling me that she never signed up to run for office. She did not choose to run. She did not name herself a leader. She smiles at my surprise. She knows I am used to modern Cherokee

politics, where so many candidates are self-ascribed leaders, not put forward in the traditional way of community call to action.

"So I went ahead. When I look back, it makes me feel good that the community did this. So I have looked up to the community since," she explains.

When days got tough, and they often do in tribal council, Marie refocused herself at the source—she returned to the old homeplace to talk with her mother. She returned to peace and simplicity and a single, native language. "Whenever we were having council and we would cover so much . . . at the end of the day . . . I would go home. I mean home where I was raised. I found that it was calming. It was like coming back down to earth. It was like slowing down. We would speak Cherokee and talk about what went on. It was a calming time—get my senses back. Language is more peaceful in the Cherokee language than it is in English." Until her passing, Marie's mother and her old homeplace served as a conduit to the peace of the language. She still goes back to the old homeplace, and of course, she plays with her eight grandchildren when her world needs more peace.

As a writer and English teacher, it goes without saying that I am fascinated with words. While I am nowhere near fluent, I enjoy learning from our Cherokee speakers and especially discussing difficult words to translate. Translation, after all, is about worldview, and quite often English and Cherokee worldviews collide. So, I was curious to ask Marie if there were any words that she had difficulty translating from Cherokee to English—that she felt like just never really rendered fully. She thought for a while. As a woman who adeptly translates legal terminology, Marie is rarely tripped up by new words and effectively uses the resources of the Language Consortium (comprised of speakers from all three Cherokee nations) to decode any tricky terms. "To-hi" (pronounced *tow he*), she finally answers. "Yes, probably that word." The basic translation of this word is *peace*, but of course, it is more than that. It is a lifestyle perspective of peace—a complete peace that requires mind, body, and spirit to be aligned. It is why Marie calls the language "peaceful." It is why so many Cherokee-speaking mothers swear that correcting a child in the Cherokee language is far more effective than the same command given in English. It is a peaceful approach that is not weak or passive. *To-hi* is an active, all-inclusive peace.

I almost hesitate to ask Marie the question I know she and other Cherokee speakers always get: "What is the future of the language?" Within that question is imbedded a connotation that it is endangered, some would even say dying. Anthropologists, linguists, and documentarians have trickled in and out of these mountains for decades fascinated with the possibility of standing in the moment, in the place, of an actual extinction. Sometimes it is as if they want to be among the last to witness it. Sometimes they want to posit a plea for rescue. Never have there been any easy answers to insuring the survival of the Cherokee language.

Marie is ready for it. She is adamant and sits up in the booth, resting her coffee on the table. "Will we save the language? Absolutely! I will not say it

is dying. I resent that statement. It is not a true statement. The [Kituwah Language] Academy has done so much. It's already beginning to live. I feel confident that it is going to live on."

When I ask her if she has any other language goals to accomplish in this lifetime, she speaks of her days of coming into the language. "I want the children to be able to read the Bible. That will be the ultimate," she relays. Marie's goal is both from a spiritual standpoint and the recognition that the Holy Bible is the most comprehensive collection of translated Cherokee vocabulary available. I think this confuses outsiders sometimes—the reliance of Christianity for Cherokee cultural perseverance. However, the text is intended to convey peace, capturing the connotation of the language more accurately than any other translated work of literature.

I joke, "To be able to write Jesus in the syllabary, right?" She laughs but expresses her wish that she could spend more time teaching her grandchildren the way her mother taught her.

"So after traveling and enjoying your time learning from others so much, what is it about this place? I mean, of course, outside this coffee shop. Why return and stay here?" I ask.

What is it about this place? Well, this is the land. Where our ancestors were. Where I was born. This is home. We are totally blessed to live in a place like this. There is no other place like it.

"What is it about this place? Well, this is the land. Where our ancestors were. Where I was born. This is home. We are totally blessed to live in a place like this. There is no other place like it," she speaks as if the answer is obvious, which I personally think it is.

After our meeting, Marie sent me an email. She had forgotten to mention a project very important to her, one that I was familiar with: the Right Path Leadership program. The Right Path, *Du-yu dv-i,* "program provides unique leadership learning that tailors contemporary leadership development competencies from the wisdom of Cherokee ancestral cultural leadership." Essentially, it translates Cherokee leadership values into modern practice. Marie's translation talents are not related to words and phrases. Translating Cherokee and English is about moving forward in the Cherokee way. It is sovereignty and cultural vitality. It is the essence of a thriving culture—change without sacrificing core values and worldview.

Marie reminds us, "When the language goes, our culture will go with it because it is all entwined." I am leaving the coffee shop with a sense of peace, though. Marie is responsible for this *to-hi*. She embodies it, and her life's work takes an active responsibility for ensuring that our history, culture, and worldview translates into the future.

There's always been a bridge here, and if Marie Junaluska has anything to say about it, there always will be.

LEE SMITH

JASON KYLE HOWARD

I t's just after 11:00 a.m. on the second day of spring, and I am back in Washington, DC, for a few days. Back in my old hometown—the place I left Kentucky for at eighteen, the place I truly came of age. It's a place I return to clear my head, to locate myself, and this visit I am locked in an internal battle with a book I am writing, one that has resurrected a legion of buried anxieties.

I am staying with an old friend out in Northern Virginia, a poet with family roots in the coalfields of Appalachia. She is at work and has left me a note on the kitchen counter reminding me to make myself at home. We are to meet that evening for a farewell dinner before I drive back to Kentucky in the morning, back to my teaching job and fear of the blank page, and after a late night of movies and talking, I am greeting the day with no definite plans. I don't need them. This is my city, a place I know as well as the hollow I was raised in, and there is never a shortage of things to do. I make myself a cup of tea to go, grab a banana, and head out the door to my car.

As I wind my way out of my friend's apartment complex, I find myself reverting to a habit I formed during my seven years of living here. I tune the radio to 88.5 WAMU, the NPR station that broadcasts from American University. And then I hear her voice.

The familiar, honeyed tones, the girlish laugh, the rippling rhythm of her speech. I cock my head in surprise, turn my right ear toward the speakers as if I might be mistaken. But I am not. She is exchanging greetings with host Diane Rehm, and I can sense her smile beaming across the airwaves as she describes how her father kept a dime store in Grundy, Virginia, and how she used to take care of the dolls, fussing over their dresses and hair while eavesdropping on the customers surrounding her.

I have missed the introduction, but I know that Rehm usually interviews her guests live in studio. I pull to the side of the road and locate the number for WAMU on my iPhone. "Hello, is Diane Rehm's interview with Lee Smith being recorded live?" I ask the woman who answers. I don't wait for her response. "Is Ms. Smith in studio?"

She pauses, perhaps to find the answer, or maybe to size me up by the sound of my voice, to intuit if I might be some rabid, unhinged fan. "Yes," she finally confirms.

In the moment it takes to offer my thanks, I am driving again, speeding, urging my Mini Cooper along the Northern Virginia backroads in the direction of Northwest DC. I have exactly fifty-five minutes to get there. To navigate the tangled mess of highways surrounding Lorton, the construction and traffic of I-95, and the curves of George Washington Parkway along the Potomac, to cross Key Bridge and disappear into the avenues and circles of the city. To find a parking place by noon and burst through the doors of WAMU to surprise Lee Smith as soon as she comes off the air.

It was her voice that beckoned me, and the voices of her characters. They were the sounds of the women I had grown up around—my mother and aunt, my living grandmother, my grandmother who died two years before I was born, all the women, young and old, in my hollow in southeastern Kentucky. Most were "world-class talkers," as Lee once described her own family, natural storytellers who conjured epics, whether from the past or from their present daily lives, that were replete with rich imagery, vernacular language, and often, poetry unawares.

I came to Lee's novels in my early twenties, when I was living in Washington. I was finally emerging from an adolescence stymied by fundamentalism, and I was being changed by the city, by its diversity of people, ideas, religions, cuisines, and landscapes. By its very air, it seemed. I was opening like a morning glory with the first graze of the sun. But sometimes

I found myself missing those voices. Their rhythm and feeling. Their sense of home, of security.

Those voices not only came alive for me in Lee's work, but they also imparted knowledge and understanding about her characters, and about the Appalachian women in my life and community. In my family, the women of generations past—and sometimes present—often found themselves without choices or options, hemmed into lives they could not escape. I recognized them in the pages of Lee's novels, and I was able to better comprehend their experiences. But I also heard whispers in her chapters, invitations to escape and understand, yes, but also to imagine. To trade places, to make substitutions. In reading her novels, I began to conjure alternative lives for the women in my family.

While reading *Fair and Tender Ladies*, I kept thinking of my maternal grandmother whom I never knew. She died two years before I was born, young and under tragic circumstances, after enduring a life colored by abuse and alcohol. Ivy Rowe allowed me to rescue her: instead of a marriage to an abusive man who won her dependence with the promise of stability, my grandmother gained new strength. She had a torrid love affair. She thumbed her nose at everyone and ran off with someone who made her deliciously happy. She was finally able to live her life on her own terms.

As I read *Saving Grace*, I was haunted by my paternal grandmother, whose life had been cloistered and subsumed by Pentecostalism, governed by a withering fear. The fear of allowing too much of the world to seep in, of letting her vulnerability show, of a slippery slope that would one day land her in the bowels of hell. In the person of Florida Grace Shepherd, my grandmother became a questioner who acknowledged the darkness and complexities of her soul.

By opening up these realms for me and her legions of other readers, I learned that Lee's voice was one to be trusted, one by which I could set my course. Dignified, inviting, probing, and vulnerable, a voice in which I have often heard the echo of my own doubts and questions.

After the initial congestion of merging onto I-95 and then sitting in traffic for a mile or so, I have finally made it to the Potomac. But I am doubting myself now, beginning to feel as if my spontaneous journey to surprise Lee is silly. I don't know why it is imperative for me to see her today, to lay eyes on her. We are supposed to be together later this summer—she has told my husband, whom she has mentored and nurtured for nearly twenty years, that she will be at the Appalachian Writers' Workshop in Hindman, Kentucky, for nearly a week, where we will all have the chance to visit, to catch up. Perhaps it's because she is in my city and I feel a duty to greet her. Perhaps it's just because of the proximity—so close it would be a shame to miss her. But no, I realize this impulse is about need, not responsibility. So I silence my fleeting reservations and focus on the road, on her voice.

As I negotiate the curve of the exit onto George Washington Parkway to follow the river north into Georgetown, Lee explains how Grundy has changed since her childhood. She describes how it was moved across the

river and out of the flood plain, and how strange it has been to return and see the new version of the town.

How did your mother and father survive the changes? Rehm asks, and I hear Lee's voice tighten. She talks about truth being stranger than fiction, about how her father died on the final day of his going-out-of-business sale in 1992 after his dime store had begun to fail. And then she says something I have heard her say before, both onstage and in conversation. That her father had declined her offer to join her in the piedmont of North Carolina. No, honey, he had said. I need me a mountain to rest my eyes against.

But it affects me differently this time, her anecdote. Outside the window, the murky Potomac is flashing past. It's windy and the river is white-capping, churning up milky crests that resemble the flashes of lace older women once tucked inside their dress sleeves. I gaze across the river, up its rolling banks to the line of cherry trees that will soon be blooming, up above their branches to the flat roof of the Lincoln Memorial, the sharpened pencil tip of the Washington Monument, the gleaming dome of the Capitol in the distance.

Lee begins to muse about Grundy. About how it has changed, how often she returns. Because she left. Like me, she was raised to leave, to fix her eyes on what lay beyond the mountains. . . .

Although I love mountains, they are not something I need—at least not every day. I prefer rivers and cityscapes, the jagged peaks of buildings and the gentle hills of the countryside to the dramatic crags that surrounded me in childhood. But there is still something in me that longs to touch wildness every once in a while, a pining to return to the landscape of my birth, to a place that is at once achingly familiar and wholly foreign to me.

I have a complicated relationship with Appalachia, with my family, and the book I am working on is demanding that I confront it. My insides are my own Potomac, roiling with this material. How, like Gracie in *Saving Grace*, I have been warped and damaged by fundamentalist religion. How, like Lee herself, I am an only child, raised by my parents to be independent. How our relationship was broken with my coming out. (*My parents, Diane, have* not *survived the changes.*) How I have been looking for home since I was eighteen, and perhaps even before.

On the radio, Lee begins to muse about Grundy. About how it has changed, how often she returns. Because she left. Like me, she was raised to leave, to fix her eyes on what lay beyond the mountains, and after earning her undergraduate degree from Hollins College, she set out on an odyssey guided by her restless spirit. Richmond, Tuscaloosa, and Nashville, then on to North Carolina: Chapel Hill and finally Hillsborough, where she settled with her husband and fellow scribe Hal Crowther, her soulmate with whom she takes annual extended sojourns to Maine and Key West, along with the occasional visit back to Grundy. I, on the other hand, rarely return to the hollow where I was raised. The place is no longer home to me—instead it is one of the places where I'm from, and there is a marked difference between the two.

As I drive, as Lee continues to talk, I wonder how long it took her to find home, to cull her options, to settle down. How she knew. I'm curious because I am in my mid-thirties and my restive impulse has persisted much longer than I imagined. Forty is looming, and I wonder where I will be— where *we* will be. I am anchored by my marriage and stepchildren. My husband and I have good, fulfilling jobs in a small college town that enable us to write. But neither of us, if we are honest, feel settled. This is not where we see ourselves in ten years, let alone twenty. This is not home.

The search for home emerges again and again in Lee's fiction, in the characters that have materialized on the pages of her legal pads. Crystal Spangler, Ivy Rowe, Florida Grace Shepherd, Evalina Touissant—they are all seekers, restless souls who carry a tortured, aching knot in their bellies. They are all homeless in a sense, wanderers who have been damaged by Appalachia as much as they have been helped.

This is because Lee Smith's Appalachia is a complex, complicated place, one that is neither romantic nor debased, but which occupies a messy, authentic middle ground. Before her emergence on the literary scene in the late 1960s, before she hit her literary stride in the 1980s, there were authors who portrayed the region with nuance. But none complexified the place like

she did by offering characters, primarily women, who wrestled with issues that arose from the region and its traditions.

In *Black Mountain Breakdown*, the first of Lee's books I ever read, Crystal Renee Spangler is gifted, popular, beautiful. The small mountain town ideal. But something goes wrong along the way. She finds herself hemmed in, no longer able to recognize her life. She cannot deal with the constrictions imposed by a conservative culture, with the trauma of an event from her past, and her mental health begins to deteriorate. She is being smothered by being what everyone expects of her and becomes an outsider to both her home and self.

Ivy Rowe is threatened by a similar type of suffocation. In *Fair and Tender Ladies*, Appalachia is portrayed as a place brimming with natural beauty that is being threatened by the expanding, exploitative coal industry. The young Ivy discovers a love for learning and writing, and she develops an active imagination that becomes her savior. She knows herself—she tends to her desires, her needs, to the natural world that surrounds her. This sturdy sense of self carries her through pregnancies, postpartum depression, and an affair with the ravishing Honey Breeding that jolts her back to life but brings with it heartrending consequences. When she is judged and exiled by her fundamentalist community, she is defiant and unapologetic. By the end of the novel, Ivy has recognized what is wonderful and terrible about the mountains, and she articulates those paradoxes. She chooses a triumphant, solitary life divorced from the oppressive elements of her culture, an Appalachia of her own making.

Home for Florida Grace Shepherd in *Saving Grace* is synonymous with both oppression and liberation. She chafes under the rules and strictures of her father's snake-handling church, but she finds freedom in the wilds of Scrabble Creek. Gracie knows she has to escape, and so she sets out on a journey that culminates in Gatlinburg, a place that seems to epitomize modern Appalachia, where natural beauty, commercialism, heritage, industry, and exploitation all converge. The ending is ambiguous: does Gracie lose it, or does she finally find herself, her home?

> *I sometimes wonder if Lee was working out her own anxieties, her own questions about home in their pages. If she realized that Appalachia is a place she will never get over.*

There is a mystery in that ending, in all of these novels, that tantalizes me. I sometimes wonder if Lee was working out her own anxieties, her own questions about home in their pages. If she realized that Appalachia is a place she will never get over. If there is a longing nestled in the crook of her heart for the rim of mountains encircling Grundy, a place about which she must have complicated feelings, a place she loves but where she could perhaps never again live.

Like Lee herself, some of her characters leave, and others stay. Some seem to be working out a question she once raised in an interview given as she was selling her childhood home in the wake of her father's death: "It's affecting me profoundly and so obviously will affect whatever I write. Just having a home to go to. What do you do when you don't have a home to go to?"

Maybe these are simply my projections. After all, we all bring our own doubts and anxieties with us to lay upon the altar of literature. But the notion of home seems to be a riddle to Crystal Spangler, to Ivy Rowe, to Florida Grace Shepherd, and perhaps it is to Lee, too. Perhaps it is to all of us.

I have crossed Key Bridge now, and I turn left into Foxhall Road, which carries me up among the lush, tamed wilds of Wesley Heights and Glover Park. Eleven years ago, I lived nearby, just three blocks from the National Cathedral and within a stone's throw of the Russian Embassy. I was twenty-three, working in communications for a federal agency, editing and writing for its magazine, and just beginning to imagine a more creative life as a writer. In many ways I was continuing the process I had begun as an eighteen-year-old at George Washington University, determining what to maintain and shed of where I was from.

I had determined that mine would be a broad life, one that gazed out at the vast expanse of the world. It would not be confined to the prisoning hills where I had been born five hundred miles away. I knew I would never again be able to live in the mountains, a realization stemming from both preference and identity. I was on the cusp of coming out, a process that had been thwarted by the fundamentalism that haunts the mountains. But I was certain I would maintain my abiding love for the region's literature, as evidenced by the worn copy of *Black Mountain Breakdown* on my bedside table. I could not only see the women of my family in those pages, but I could also see myself in Crystal Spangler: the overachieving student who carried the confining expectations of her community on her slender shoulders and was destroyed by them. Crystal was my cautionary tale—I would never find myself imprisoned by a life not of my own making.

As I drive past Garfield Street, the turn I would have made to my old home with its shelf of Appalachian novels, I laugh at the memory, at my youthful inflation of my own power. At the fact that although I have succeeded in living broadly, my life has assumed a confining propulsion of its own centered on home, one I haven't quite been able to control as I thought I would. At the irony that it was Appalachian literature that helped take

me back to Kentucky, although not to the mountains, and that the words of Lee Smith and Silas House, my future husband, actually helped to beckon me back west.

But since then, some of my certainties have vanished. The hollow I was raised in has descended into rampant drug abuse. Beloved community members have died; others have moved away. Some have latched onto a vicious brand of conservatism that I cannot begin to understand or respect.

My lapsed Southern Baptist parents have become fervent Pentecostals. They don't accept me or my family, and I no longer have a childhood home to which I feel I can return. Everything, it seems, has changed.

On the air, Lee has just finished explaining Grundy's three-story Walmart, replete with its escalators that transport customers and their shopping carts, a description prompted by a caller from Louisville who had once visited and left amazed. Then Diane Rehm makes an announcement. An email has come in from Wesley, whose location is not given. "May I object to the nostalgia for a time that never really existed?" Wesley asks. "While Ms. Smith enjoyed a childhood she remembers as idyllic, others in her city were denied an equal education or access to jobs."

I raise up erect behind the wheel, bristling at Wesley's implication. Not about Appalachia's racial or class disparities—he is exactly right about this and is, in fact, making an important point—but at the assumption he seems to be making about Lee. That she is engaging in mere nostalgia. That her memoir, her body of work, is sentimental drivel and doesn't portray Appalachia's complications. It's an accusation often thrown at women, that their work simply is not gritty enough. That it's mere flummery, something that Lee Smith's writing surely is not. Lee handles the moment with her customary grace and moves on.

My blood has simmered back down as I reach Tenleytown and American University. I am nearing WAMU, having made it earlier than expected. The traffic gods have been kind, I think. I pull into the lot behind the Metro station and exit the car when I realize there is a problem. WAMU is no longer here. As soon as I see the building and the suite advertising its new tenant, I remember reading about the move on social media.

I check the time: 11:45. I find the address of the new location over on Connecticut Avenue, and by the time I return to my car I have already plotted my route to the new studio through the backstreets. Back down Wisconsin to Tenley Circle, around to Albermarle Street and then southeast on Connecticut.

Lee is talking about her novel *Saving Grace*, about how Florida Grace is born into a conservative, religious home from which she ultimately attempts to run. I am only half-hearing now, because there is construction on Albermarle, and I am forced to reroute. But I know the story.

Community, I hear Lee say. Home.

That word again. I turn it over in my mind as I drive down 38th Street to Alton Place, where I am greeted by another detour. So I reroute: 38th again to Yuma, then south on Reno before making a left on Van Ness.

Perhaps Wesley is right, though not about Lee. Maybe *I* am the one being nostalgic and sentimental, idealizing a fixed notion of home that really does not exist, or at least no longer does. Or maybe we all take detours, and some of those are pointing us toward our destination on city side streets. When I finally reach Connecticut, Lee and Diane Rehm are wrapping up their chat.

———

Great literature asks questions. It asks them of characters, and by extension, it demands we ask them of ourselves. Like most lifelong readers, I realized this at a young age—that my questions were welcomed by literature, and sometimes even answered by it. When I discovered Lee's writing, I found that her novels were no exception, and I began turning to them for answers about where I was from. Because there are questions raised in her writing about Appalachia—important ones, queries posed by her characters and their lives.

How has conservatism in the Mountain South constrained women over the years? How does the region judge and sentence people—again, often women—who refuse to conform to proscribed social norms? How and where does beauty persist in a natural world threatened by industry? How does religious fundamentalism thwart creativity and spiritual growth? Is Appalachia a place where people who are different can ultimately live?

These are not nostalgic, sentimental questions. These are interrogations, difficult questions that challenge power dynamics and structures in Appalachia and throughout the South, including patriarchy, religion, industrialism, prejudice. Lee asks these on the page with subtlety, with her trademark depth and nuance, and her asking never interferes with the art or the telling of the story. But in posing these questions through her characters, she is doing something else as well. She is opening a world for her readers, a universe void of judgment, in which she gives them permission to ask those very questions of themselves, to apply them to their own lives.

Such openness, at its core, is an act of inherent generosity, which might be the first word that comes to mind when I think of Lee. Both on the page and in her own life, she has come to exemplify what it means to give of herself not only to her readers, but also to her fellow writers. An entire generation of Appalachian and Southern writers can trace their roots back to her work, encouragement, and patronage.

What she has given these writers, and scores of others, is permission to follow our creative impulses, a sanction that is rooted in belief. The belief that anything is possible, that we have a responsibility to lead examined lives. "I refuse to lead an unexamined life," I have heard her say on more than one occasion, advice I have scrawled on a note card and taped above my writing desk. In *Dimestore*, Lee adds a vital addendum: "No matter how painful it may be, I want to know what's going on."

That is our duty as writers. To keep asking, to keep examining, to keep searching. The quest is its own reward, itself a kind of home. This I have gathered from her work. From her, our North Star—or better yet, our bright, constant Southern star. A generous, open-hearted literary refuge toward which we can all steer our speeding cars.

After the traffic and construction; after going to the old, wrong location; after the crooked detour on the closed backstreets; I find a parking place just a block away from WAMU's posh new headquarters. It is 12:05 p.m. I push some coins into the meter and tear off down the sidewalk toward the studio. By the time I heave open the doors and thrust myself into the lobby, adrenaline and sprinting have conspired to make me a sweaty mess. A touch of my childhood asthma has reappeared in my dash through the cold air, and I have to pause to catch my breath before approaching the receptionist at her desk on the right side of the lobby.

"Hello, is Lee Smith still here?" I inquire.

"It's you," she smiles. "You called earlier."

"I did. Have I missed her?"

She points over my shoulder. "She's right in there."

I turn to see an expansive, glass-enclosed conference room. Lee is standing with her back to me, talking to another woman I don't recognize. A couple of other women are sitting at a table, engrossed in conversation.

I approach the glass wall and knock. Everyone is startled, bewildered, and I don't care. I need to see Lee.

She turns around and I wave through the glass. Her eyes become the size of egg yolks.

"Oh my God!" I hear her laugh, and I burst through the door to give her a hug.

"What are you doing here?" she asks.

I begin to explain, and when I see that lovely smile bloom across her face, I know why I am here—why I need Lee Smith to rest my eyes against. As she erupts in laughter at the tale of my tortured journey to find her, I know all will be well. I know my book will be fine. I know my husband and I will someday find our home. I know that goodness and generosity still persist in this world. And I know there will always be an Appalachia—the one she has conjured—to which I can return over and over again, a home on the page in which I can see myself and love without condition.

CONTRIBUTORS

Tanya Amyx Berry is a photographer, artist, and agrarian who shares a hillside farm with her husband, Wendell Berry. Her work includes her book of photographs *For the Hog Killing, 1979.*

Mallory Cash is an editorial and portrait photographer based in Wilmington, North Carolina. Her work has appeared in the Knoxville Museum of Art, *Salt Magazine, Dear Photographer Magazine,* the *New York Times, Encore Magazine, O'Henry Magazine, Garden & Gun, Our State, Pine-Straw Magazine, Bold Life,* and has been or will be featured in galleries in Tennessee, Virginia, and West Virginia.

Wiley Cash is the *New York Times* best-selling author of the novels *The Last Ballad, A Land More Kind Than Home,* and *This Dark Road to Mercy.* The founder of the Open Canon Book Club and the cofounder of the Land More Kind Appalachian Artists' Residency, he serves as the writer-in-residence at the University of North Carolina–Asheville and teaches in the Mountainview Low-Residency MFA. He lives with his wife and two young daughters in North Carolina.

Annette Saunooke Clapsaddle, an enrolled member of the Eastern Band of Cherokee Indians (EBCI), resides in Qualla, North Carolina. She holds degrees from Yale University and the College of William and Mary. Her debut novel, *Even as We Breathe* is scheduled to release summer of 2020. Her first novel manuscript, *Going to Water,* is winner of the Morning Star Award for Creative Writing from the Native American Literature Symposium (2012) and a finalist for the PEN/Bellwether Prize for Socially Engaged Fiction (2014). After serving as executive director of the Cherokee Preservation Foundation, Annette returned to teaching English and Cherokee Studies at Swain County High School. She is coeditor of the *Journal of Cherokee Studies* and serves on the board of trustees for the North Carolina Writers Network. In addition to reading and writing, Annette enjoys playing basketball, mountain biking, and hiking.

Amy D. Clark is a native of Jonesville, Virginia. She is the editor/author of two books and several articles and essays. Clark's writing has appeared in the *New York Times*, NPR, and *Salon*, among many other publications. Clark's coedited book, *Talking Appalachian: Voice, Identity, and Community*, was used as a dialect resource for actors during the filming of *Big Stone Gap*, a movie adaptation of Adriana Trigiani's novel of the same title, and she also served as a dialect consultant on the film's script. Her writing has won the Lamar York Prize for Nonfiction, a fellowship to the Key West Literary Seminar, and recognition in *Best American Essays*. Clark chairs the Communication Studies department at the University of Virginia's College at Wise, where she codirects the Center for Appalachian Studies.

Tim C. Cox is a communicative photographer hailing from small-town Virginia. In his fifty-three-year career, he has focused his lens on a multitude of subjects and topics, but the true art is in the attention to even the smallest details to narrate the photographic story from beginning to end.

Amy Greene's first novel *Bloodroot* was a *New York Times* and National Bestseller. In 2010 Greene won the Weatherford Award for Appalachian Fiction. Her second novel, *Long Man*, was a *Washington Post* Top Book of the Year for 2014. In 2016 Greene won the Willie Morris Award for Southern Literature and was inducted into the East Tennessee Literary Hall of Fame. Her essays have appeared in the *New York Times* and *Glamour Magazine*, among other publications.

Silas House is the nationally best-selling author of five novels—*Clay's Quilt*, *A Parchment of Leaves*, *The Coal Tattoo*, *Eli the Good*, and *Same Sun Here* (coauthored with Neela Vaswani)—a book of creative nonfiction, *Something's Rising*, coauthored with Jason Kyle Howard; and three plays: *The Hurting Part*, *This Is My Heart for You*, and *In These Fields*, with Sam

Gleaves. He is a member of the Fellowship of Southern Writers, the recipient of three honorary doctorates, and the winner of the Nautilus Award, an EB White Award, the Appalachian Book of the Year, the Jesse Stuart Award, the Lee Smith Award, and many other honors. House serves on the fiction faculty at the Spalding MFA in Creative Writing and as the NEH Chair at Berea College.

Jason Kyle Howard is the award-winning author, coauthor, or editor of three acclaimed books: *A Few Honest Words: The Kentucky Roots of Popular Music, Something's Rising: Appalachians Fighting Mountaintop Removal,* and *We All Live Downstream: Writing about Mountaintop Removal.* Howard has written numerous essays that have been widely anthologized and have appeared in the *New York Times, The Nation, Sojourners,* and several other publications. A southeastern Kentucky native, Howard holds a BA in Political Communication from The George Washington University, an MA in history from the University of Kentucky, and an MFA in creative writing from Vermont College of Fine Arts.

Patricia Hudson, an eighth-generation East Tennessean, has been a freelance writer for thirty-five years. She spent a decade as a contributing editor for *Americana Magazine* and has been a regular contributor to *Southern Living.* Her book credits include a volume in the *Smithsonian Guide to Historic America* and the anthology *Listen Here: Women Writing in Appalachia.* In 2005, she cofounded the environmental group LEAF to fight mountaintop removal coal mining in Tennessee. Hudson holds an MFA from Spalding University.

Karen Salyer McElmurray is an American writer of literary fiction, creative nonfiction, and memoir. She is the author of *The Motel of the Stars, Surrendered Child: A Birth Mother's Journey,* and *Strange Birds in the Tree of Heaven,* as well as numerous essays and short stories. McElmurray was Editor's Pick by *Oxford American* in November 2009 and was the recipient of the AWP Creative Nonfiction award in 2003. McElmurray has received numerous literary awards and has served at numerous colleges and universities as an instructor, professor, and writer-in-residence.

Guy Mendes's photographs have appeared in *Aperture, Newsweek,* the *Smithsonian, Mother Jones,* the *New York Times, Garden & Gun, Southern Accents, Bomb,* and the quarterlies *Parnassus* and *Conjunctions.* He has exhibited at the International Center for Photography, the Aperture Gallery, the New Orleans Museum of Art, the High Museum, the University of Kentucky Art Museum, the University of Louisville Photographic Archives, the Speed Art Museum, Zephyr Gallery, and the Kentucky Museum of Art and Design.

Robert Morton is a photographer and videographer based in Lexington, Kentucky. Born in Los Angeles and raised in Kentucky, he graduated from Eastern Kentucky University with a degree in Broadcasting and Electronic Media. His work has been published by Yahoo News, BET, *The Shade Room,* and other outlets.

Shawn Poynter is a commercial and editorial photographer based in Knoxville, Tennessee. He specializes in reportage, portraiture, and travel photography and has been featured in the *New York Times, ABC Nightline,* the *Los Angeles Times, Chicago Tribune, Washington Post,* and *Sierra* magazine, among many other national publications and outlets.

Sam Stapleton is a fine-art photographer based in Knoxville, Tennessee, who recently published a collection of his photographs, *Stilled Life* (2018). His work has been exhibited in galleries across the Southeast, as well as in Portland, Oregon, and Chicago, Illinois. Stapleton's works have also appeared in books and magazines such as *Rich Community: An Anthology of Appalachian Photographers, Inns of the Southern Mountains,* and *CaptureMania Magazine.*

Tasha Thomas is a North Carolina–based photographer with strong ties to Tennessee and Texas as well. She spent years hiring photographers as the art director for Sugar Hill Records and is now enjoying her time behind the camera. She specializes in portraiture (both people and pets) and nature/wildlife photography.

Will Warasila is a photographer based in Durham, North Carolina, and Brooklyn, New York. He is an MFA candidate in Experimental and Documentary Arts at Duke University. His work has appeared in *Atmos*, *ACID MAG*, *Bloomberg Businessweek*, *Interview Magazine*, the *New Yorker*, the *New York Times*, *Vice*, *WAX*, *Wired*, and elsewhere.

C. Williams is a multifaceted artist—photographer, production designer, and art director for commercials and film. She is also a writer, focused on fiction and screenwriting. She cowrote a short narrative film, *The Story of Uncle Nearest*, that debuted at Tribeca Film Institute in February 2019. Her short stories have been published in the *Louisville Review*, *Pikeville Review*, *Still: The Journal*, and *Appalachian Heritage*. Her photographs have also been published in both *Still: The Journal* and as cover images for *Appalachian Heritage*. The GAC (Great American Country) Corporation purchased a collection of more than forty of her Nashville-based photographs to feature in their Nashville headquarters. C. Williams is happily based in Nashville, on the East Side.